J B PATRICK
Mello, Tara Baukus.
Danica Patrick /
ALPA

DANICA PATRICK

RACE CAR LEGENDS

COLLECTOR'S EDITION

A.J. Foyt

The Allisons

Dale Earnhardt Jr.

Danica Patrick

Famous Finishes

Famous Tracks

The Jarretts

Jeff Burton

Jeff Gordon

Jimmie Johnson

Kenny Irwin Jr.

The Labonte Brothers

Lowriders

Mario Andretti

Mark Martin

Monster Trucks & Tractors

Motorcycles

The Need for Speed

Off-Road Racing

The Pit Crew

Rockcrawling

Rusty Wallace

Stunt Driving

Tony Stewart

The Unsers

DANICA PATRICK

Tara Baukus Mello

CHELSEA HOUSE
PUBLISHERS
An imprint of Infobase Publishing

Danica Patrick

Copyright © 2008 by Infobase Publishing

Chelsea House
An imprint of Infobase Publishing
132 West 31st Street
New York NY 10001

ISBN-10: 0-7910-9126-0
ISBN-13: 978-0-7910-9126-5

Library of Congress Cataloging-in-Publication Data
Mello, Tara Baukus.
 Danica Patrick / Tara Baukus Mello.
   p. cm. – (Race car legends. Collector's edition)
 Includes bibliographical references and index.
 ISBN 0-7910-9126-0 (hardcover)
 1. Patrick, Danica, 1982 2. Automobile racing drivers—United States—
Biography—Juvenile literature. 3. Women automobile racing drivers—
United States—Biography—Juvenile literature. I. Title. II. Series.
GV1032.P38M45 2007   796.72092—dc22
[B]   2006035154

Chelsea House books are available at special discounts when purchased in bulk quantities for businesses, associations, institutions, or sales promotions. Please call our Special Sales Department in New York at (212) 967-8800 or (800) 322-8755.

You can find Chelsea House books on the World Wide Web at
http://www.chelseahouse.com

Series design by Erika K. Arroyo
Cover design by Hierophant Publishing Services/EON PreMedia/Jooyoung An

Printed in the United States of America

Bang PH 10 9 8 7 6 5 4 3 2 1

This book is printed on acid-free paper.

All links and Web addresses were checked and verified to be correct at the time of publication. Because of the dynamic nature of the Web, some addresses and links may have changed since publication and may no longer be valid.

CONTENTS

1

TURNING HEADS

The Indianapolis 500—or the Indy 500, for short—is perhaps the most famous of all automobile races held in the United States. More than 350,000 people arrive at the Indianapolis Motor Speedway on race day to watch the competition. Teams who are hoping to compete will arrive in Indianapolis, Indiana, one month before the big race. During that month, they practice and test everything, and eventually make an attempt to qualify for one of the 33 positions available on race day. This time of preparation is known as "the month of May" in racing circles.

One of the drivers who was in town for the month of May in 2005 was Danica Patrick, a 23-year-old **rookie** in the **Indy Racing League,** or IRL. Patrick had caught the attention of race fans, as well as her competitors, because she was a woman competing in a sport made up almost entirely of men. At least that's what they noticed in the beginning. But soon there was something else very important to notice about Danica Patrick: She was a strong competitor on the track.

In just four races in the 2005 racing season, Patrick had already proved that she could race. Each time she climbed into the driver's seat at the Indianapolis Motor Speedway,

Indy Racing League rookie Danica Patrick speeds out of the pit area as the first car on the track to start practice at the Indianapolis Motor Speedway on May 8, 2005.

also known as the Brickyard, people stopped to watch. About halfway through the month of May, Patrick really gave everyone something to see. On May 12, 2005, she

BUILDING THE BRICKYARD

The Indianapolis Motor Speedway was built in 1909. The surface of the track was originally made of crushed rock and tar, but this proved to be too slippery for racing. To fix it, the track owners brought in 3.2 million bricks from western Indiana. They laid them on the two-mile oval track in late summer 1909. Thanks to its new track, the speedway quickly became known as the Brickyard. But throughout the years, race cars became much faster, so driving over a brick track became a much bumpier ride. Portions of the brick track were paved over with asphalt. By 1961, almost all of the bricks had been covered. Today, only three feet of bricks remain at the start/finish line.

logged the fastest time—227.633 miles per hour—of all the drivers in practice.

Suddenly, it seemed as though everyone was talking about this petite brunette. Fans recognized her almost everywhere she went and asked for her autograph. By the time she and the other 32 Indy 500 drivers traveled to New York City to promote the upcoming race, Patrick was well on her way to becoming a name that everyone in the country recognized. During a single day on that New York City trip, Patrick did 27 television interviews, 9 radio interviews and more than a dozen interviews with reporters for newspapers and magazines. In the week before the race, the newspaper *USA Today* wrote two articles about her, and both of them appeared on the front page.

It was attention that was well deserved, because Patrick was the fourth-fastest driver in the race's **qualifying rounds**. It was the highest starting position of any woman to compete in the Indy 500. Still, Patrick did not let the success go to her head. Just before the race she said, "Everybody loves to go for the underdog and I am [the underdog]. I am the rookie."

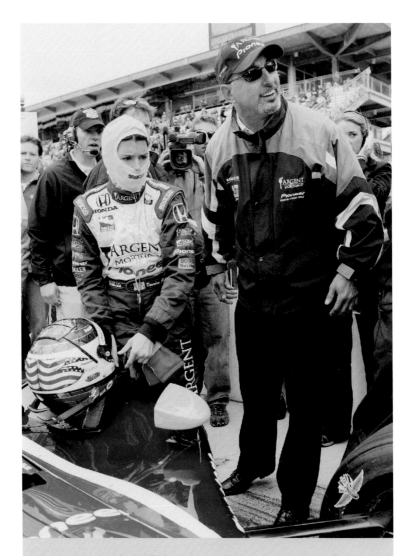

Car owner Bobby Rahal (*right*) smiles as Danica Patrick removes her helmet after qualifying for the 2005 Indianapolis 500 with an average speed of 227.004 miles per hour.

Everyone, including Patrick, knew it would be a challenge for a rookie to win the Indy 500. But everyone also knew it was not impossible. In fact, many racing experts called Patrick the favorite to win. She not only had the driving skills needed, but she also had two other important pieces in the puzzle: a fast car and an experienced team. Patrick knew that these items were extremely important. She said, "I think the first thing you need is a good team. You need good strategy, you need good **pit stops**, you need people with a clear idea of what needs to happen out there."

BREAKING BARRIERS

On May 29, 2005, Patrick became the fourth woman to compete in the Indy 500. That in itself was an accomplishment. The first Indy 500 was held in 1911; and up until the 1970s, no women were allowed at the track except as spectators. In all that time, only one exception was made. That exception was for Denise McCluggage, a race car driver and journalist who was let into the press box to cover the race in 1956. This happened after a supportive male reporter from *The New York Times* threatened to leave if she was excluded.

All areas of the Indianapolis Motor Speedway, including the garage, pits and press box, were opened to women in 1971, after a female reporter filed a lawsuit and won. Six years later, in 1977, a successful road racer named Janet Guthrie became the first woman to compete in the famous race.

Just like Patrick, Guthrie captured the attention of race fans as well as the media. During the month of May in 1977, Guthrie was on the front page of five major newspapers and did many television interviews, including for *The Today Show*. While many people were supportive of Guthrie's accomplishment of qualifying for the race, not everyone was entirely comfortable with a woman racing in the Indy 500. That included the owner of the Indianapolis Motor Speedway, Tony Hulman.

Janet Guthrie's pit crew congratulates her following her finish in the 1978 Indianapolis 500. Guthrie is the first woman ever to have completed the race.

Hulman was the one who made famous the phrase, "Gentlemen, start your engines!" With Guthrie competing in the Indy 500, everyone wanted to know what Hulman was going to say. He said that he was considering using the word "Gentlemen" in the race anyway "because after all, it's the mechanics who start the engines." When race day arrived, however, Hulman found a way to show his respect, while keeping tradition at the same time. He said, "In company with the first lady ever to qualify at Indianapolis— gentlemen, start your engines."

In 2005, 28 years after Guthrie made history by becoming the first woman to compete in the Indy 500, Patrick was hoping to make history of her own: She was hoping to win. At noon on race day, Mari Hulman George, Tony Hulman's daughter and the chairman of the board of the Indianapolis Motor Speedway at that time, started the race by saying, "Lady and gentlemen, start your engines!"

PUSHING FOR A WIN

On lap 57 of the race, Patrick made history by moving into the lead. It was the first time ever that a woman had led a lap in the Indy 500. In fact, Patrick led for a total of 19 laps that day. Things continued to go well for her until she went in for a pit stop on lap 79. When it was time for her to leave the pits, she stalled the car. To restart it, one of her crewmembers had to get the team's large starter box and attach it to the back of her car. Precious seconds were lost, and by the time she returned to the racetrack, she had dropped to sixteenth place.

Patrick knew she had a lot of ground to make up, and she slowly began working her way through the field of cars. By lap 147 of the 200-lap race, she was in ninth place. At the

Danica Patrick's crew hurriedly restarts her car engine after it stalled during a pit stop on lap 79 of the Indianapolis 500 on May 29, 2005.

next **caution flag**, many of the racers, including Patrick, went in for a pit stop. Patrick's team performed fast work, and when she left the pits on lap 156, she was in eighth place. IRL rules required Patrick to keep her position until the green flag was waved to restart the race.

When the race started again, Patrick stepped hard on the **accelerator** pedal. Before she knew it, her tires lost their grip on the track, and her car spun, hitting rookie driver Tomas Enge and damaging the front of her vehicle. The damage meant that Patrick needed to go in for another pit stop right away so that her team could replace the **nose cone** of her race car.

The crowd goes wild as Danica Patrick passes Dan Wheldon to take the lead on a restart at lap 190 of the 2005 Indy 500.

When she rejoined the race, Patrick had fallen again to ninth place; but she took the lead again on lap 172, when the race leaders went in for their pit stops. Patrick held the lead for 14 laps, until lap 186, when Dan Wheldon passed her. Wheldon kept the lead for only a short time, though. Another caution flag flew, and when the race restarted on lap 190, Patrick was able again to take the lead.

With just 10 laps left in the race, it looked as though Patrick had a very real chance of being the first woman to win the Indianapolis 500. The spectators in the grandstands were on their feet and cheering so loudly that Patrick's fiancé, Paul Hospenthal, said that he couldn't hear the cars. Unfortunately, Patrick's chief engineer, Ray Leto, knew something that the crowd did not: All of her fast driving meant that she didn't have enough fuel to continue to stay hard on the accelerator and maintain her lead. And, with just a few laps left in the race, there wasn't time for Patrick to go into the pits to refuel.

Her crew told her the news over the radio, and Patrick began to go easy on the accelerator. Soon, Wheldon passed her. Patrick's teammate, Vitor Meira, came next, followed by Wheldon's teammate, Bryan Herta. In the end, Patrick finished in fourth place, the same place in which she had started. "Wow, what a race for me," Patrick said afterwards. "I think I showed that I was a rookie with some of the things that happened. But I think I showed that my on-track performance is all there. I got to lead the race in my first Indy 500 and actually had a chance to win the race. I am pleased with my performance today and all month [in practice]."

Patrick's strong showing at the 89th Annual Indianapolis 500 not only made her more popular, but it also brought many new fans to the sport of IndyCar racing. Television ratings for the race were 59 percent higher than they were in 2004. In May 2005 alone, more Danica Patrick merchandise (such as T-shirts and models of her car) was sold than the amount of merchandise sold for all of the other IRL drivers combined in the history of the league. Although Patrick was turning more heads than ever before, it wasn't the first time she would be in the spotlight. And it definitely wouldn't be the last.

2

GROWING UP ON THE TRACK

Danica Sue Patrick was born on March 25, 1982. She grew up in Roscoe, Illinois, about 100 miles northwest of Chicago. Her dad, T.J., and mom, Bev, have always been interested in racing. Before Danica was born, her father raced snowmobiles, dirt bikes, and **Midget** cars on a dirt track. Danica's parents first met at a snowmobile race where Bev was the mechanic for a female snowmobile racer.

When Danica was growing up, her parents owned a glass company, cutting glass for windows and mirrors. Being the owner of a company meant that T.J. Patrick spent long hours away from Danica and her younger sister, Brooke. When Danica was 10 and Brooke was 8, the Patricks decided that they needed to have a family hobby to help them spend more time together. They wanted something that all of them could participate in, so they decided to start racing go-karts.

At first, Brooke was very interested in racing go-karts, and Danica decided she wanted to race because her sister was racing. The Patricks outfitted both of their daughters

Danica Patrick receives a hug from her mother, Bev. Patrick's parents, Beverly and T.J. Patrick, started Danica and her sister go-kart racing as a family hobby in 1992.

with the necessary racing gear, and they all went to their first race. It turned out that Brooke didn't like racing that much, and Danica loved it. This surprised Danica's parents because in that very first race, she crashed her

A GO-KART START

Patrick got her racing start in go-karts. A go-kart driver sits in a seat on top of the vehicle's frame. A go-kart has no body—the metal shell made up of the roof, the sides of a vehicle, and its hood. Go-karts weigh about 150 pounds, not counting the driver, and are powered by small motors similar to the engine on a lawn mower. There are two types of go-karts for competition: sprint and enduro. Patrick raced sprint go-karts, which are the most common. Sprint go-kart races are usually run on paved tracks of one-quarter to one-half of a mile long. Kids can begin competing at age 8 and continue racing until age 16.

IndyCar Rookie of the Year, Danica Patrick, races a go-kart at an event in Union Square Park in New York on October 20, 2005.

go-kart into a wall at 25 mph after its brakes didn't work. The crash scared Danica's parents. Her dad said, "I thought I had killed her." But Danica wasn't hurt. In fact, she couldn't wait to get back out on the track. She later said, "I knew I would have to concentrate, improve, and be determined, but racing is something I wanted to do once I drove that kart for the first time." Danica did improve; and by the end of the year, she finished in second place out of 20 drivers.

Although Brooke raced for only a few months before deciding it wasn't right for her, 1992 was the start of Danica's racing career. By age 12, she had won her first championship, the World Karting Association's Grand National Championship in the Yamaha Sportsman class. That championship made Danica realize that racing could be an actual career. She began to dream that perhaps one day she could compete in the Indianapolis 500. Little did she know that her dream would come true just 11 years later.

Danica Patrick and her younger sister, Brooke (*left*), watch the racing action at the Indianapolis Motor Speedway.

Danica raced in different go-kart classes for five years, and she won—a lot. She still found time for other activities, though. She was on the basketball and volleyball teams at school, played the flute in her school band, and sang in the choir. In junior high and high school, she was a cheerleader. Yet with all these other activities, racing was still her favorite.

THE BIG MOVE

When she was 16, it was time for Danica to take the next step in her racing career and move from go-karts to race cars. She attended the Formula Ford racing school in Canada and then moved by herself to England, where she competed in the Formula Vauxhall Winter Series.

The decision for Danica to move to England wasn't hard, because she and her family knew that it was the right choice if she wanted a career in racing. Bev Patrick explained, "If you want to be the best lawyer, you go to Harvard. If you want to be the best driver, you go to England." Just the same, her family would miss her terribly. And Danica had to give up not just her family, but also all of her friends from high school and activities like cheerleading and her prom. Before she moved, she received what is called a general equivalency diploma, a certificate worth about the same as a high school diploma, given to people who take a special test instead of finishing school. That was the end of her formal schooling.

In 1999, Patrick competed in her first full season in Formula Vauxhall and finished ninth in the race for the championship. British formula car racing is considered one of the most difficult and most competitive series in all of racing, so everyone thought finishing in the top 10 in her first year was an accomplishment. It was Danica's first time behind the wheel of a serious race car, and she was regularly driving at speeds faster than 200 miles per hour.

Although the experience was thrilling, it was also difficult. Her fellow drivers were all men, and they were not ready to welcome a woman to their group. Patrick later said, "All the drivers hung out together, and I was left out of the equation a lot. They wouldn't call me. It was boys being boys." The fact that the other drivers didn't accept her was also a problem on the track. In qualifying rounds, drivers often work with other drivers to create **drafting**, which allows two cars to go faster than each could if it were traveling alone. Danica had a harder time qualifying because none of the other drivers would allow her to draft them.

In 2000, she moved up to the next level in formula racing and competed in the British Zetek Formula Ford Championship. Patrick recalled, "I knew if I was going to reach goals like **Formula One** or **CART** Champ Cars, I needed to race in British Formula Ford. The series has some of the best wheel-to-wheel racing in the world. I knew I would improve my skills by racing in that series."

Moving up to this series was a challenge for Patrick. There was a lot for her to learn. By the time the last race of the season arrived, Patrick proved she had learned a lot. Luck came her way when another, more experienced driver on her team got a new race car toward the end of the season. Patrick was given his old one to drive, a car of much higher quality than her previous vehicle. With the better equipment, Patrick could drive even faster.

The last race was also the biggest race of the year: the Formula Ford Festival. Patrick was the only woman to compete in the event. Out of the 28 drivers who made it through the preliminary races, Patrick started ninth. She quickly moved her way through the pack of cars. When the checkered flag dropped, signaling that the first-place driver had crossed the finish line, she was in second place, just a half second behind the winner. It was the best finish by any woman in the history of the race. It also matched the best effort ever by any American driver. Danny Sullivan, an Indy 500 winner and a CART champion, had also placed second in the race in 1974.

HOMECOMING

The following year, 2001, Patrick had hoped to move up to the next level of the racing series, called Formula Three. Unfortunately, she wasn't able to get enough sponsorship money to let her race competitively. In addition to being a good race car driver, it is very important to have a race car that is built by the most skilled workmen so that it is as fast and strong as possible. It is also a good idea to have many extra race car parts handy during a race. All of that takes money, and for Formula Three, it takes a lot of money.

Because Patrick did not have enough sponsorship money to race in Formula Three (and besides that, she missed her family), she decided it was time to return to the United States. As she looked for a team owner who would support her in an **open-wheel** car in the United States, she tested in several different kinds of cars. The year 2002 was filled with more testing, in addition to competing in a few races in the Barber Dodge Pro Series.

In 2002, Patrick also competed in the Long Beach Grand Prix Toyota Pro/Celebrity race. Among the competitors are professional race car drivers and celebrities

Danica Patrick takes the lead during a Barber Dodge Pro Series race in Vancouver, Canada, in July 2002.

who often have some racing experience; the sponsor, Toyota, specifically invites all of the drivers to the race. Some of the people whom Patrick competed against that year included Olympic champion Dara Torres, comedian and actor Chris Titus, and fellow racers Sarah Fisher and Tommy Kendall. All of the racers competed in identical Toyota Celicas, and the race was held on the closed streets of downtown Long Beach, California.

Patrick thought the race was going to be easy, but she discovered in the qualifying rounds that it was going to be a bit more challenging than she had thought. After qualifying she said, "I thought I'd run right past the celebrities, but they did a good job. Tommy Kendall, now that guy is going to be my challenge. But I think I can beat him!"

Pro/Celebrity race winners Dara Torres (*left*) and Danica Patrick wave to fans as they take their victory lap at the Toyota Grand Prix in Long Beach, California, in April 2002.

And beat him she did. Patrick finished first in the Pro category in the race. It was good practice, because the very next year, Patrick would be back to race on the streets of Long Beach for her first full season of professional racing in the United States.

3

✖✖✖✖✖✖✖✖

GETTING SERIOUS

After 11 years of racing, Patrick got her first full-time ride, or job, in a professional racing series in the United States in 2003. Bobby Rahal, a former Indy 500 winner, was by this time a race team owner. Rahal not only hired Patrick, but he also formed a Toyota Atlantic race team just for her. Although Rahal owned other teams, it was the first time he was involved with this racing series.

Patrick and Rahal first met at a race in Wisconsin and then met again in England, when they were both living there. Rahal was in England working for the car company Jaguar on its Formula One racing program. He followed Patrick's efforts as she raced British open-wheel cars and was impressed. "[British open-wheel racing] is the most intense environment in the world for young drivers to try to get to Formula One," Rahal told a newspaper reporter in 2003.

When Patrick returned to the United States, Rahal was so impressed with her racing ability that he hired her. He decided she should compete in the CART Toyota Atlantic Championship series, an open-wheel racing series that less experienced drivers go into before moving onto the

Bobby Rahal, former race car driver and winner of the 1986 Indianapolis 500, watches practice at the Indianapolis Motor Speedway in 2002 for the first time as a car owner. In 2003, Rahal formed a Toyota Atlantic race team and gave Danica Patrick her first full-time ride.

Champ Car World Series. Other famous race car drivers who competed in Toyota Atlantic racing include Michael Andretti, Paul Tracy, and Sam Hornish Jr.

The announcement that Patrick would be racing in the series generated a lot of attention because it was the first time in the 30-year history of the series that a woman would race full time. Some people wondered whether Patrick could be a strong competitor because she was a woman. Rahal responded by saying, "This isn't a publicity stunt.

My reputation, name and everything I've done in racing is on the line. I wouldn't have done this if I didn't think she could do it."

READY TO RACE

At the first race of the 2003 season, Patrick was all set to show everyone that she could be a competitor. She qualified fifth out of 15 drivers for the Tecate/Telmex Monterrey Grand Prix, held in Monterrey, Mexico. Patrick's qualifying lap time was just a little more than a half-second slower than the **pole position** winner Luis Diaz, and Patrick thought she could have been even faster. "On the last lap, we ran out of fuel, and we were actually two-tenths faster than our fast lap" she explained. "Who knows where we would have ended up?"

On race day, Patrick and her team were ready. Early on in the race, Luis Diaz and the third-place qualifier, rookie A.J. Allmendinger, bumped each other, causing both men to lose their good positions. Second-place qualifier Joey Hand took the lead, but he didn't keep it for long. Michael Valiante, who started fourth, overtook him in lap 6. Soon, Hand began to have mechanical problems with his car that caused him to leave the race. Jonathan Macri, who started sixth, passed Patrick. By lap 12, he had moved into second place, with Patrick close behind. Both Macri and Patrick chased Valiante, but neither was able to catch him. In the end, Patrick finished third, behind Valiante and Macri.

Patrick's third-place finish went down in the books as the highest finish for a woman in the history of the Toyota Atlantic series. After the race, Patrick said, "I didn't have a good enough car to get by Jonathan, and I started to understeer [slide to the outside of the track while going

Danica Patrick stands by her car as she waits for a qualifying race to begin during the 2003 racing season.

through turns] halfway through the race and I ran out of adjustments. . . . In the end, the car was great. I think it was a reflection of how a lot of people have been working as a team at Team Rahal. We're just excited."

Although Patrick had started the 2003 season on a good note, she was still a rookie in Toyota Atlantic racing, which meant that there was a lot to learn. In the following 10 races of the season, Patrick had three more top 5 finishes, but she also had two crashes that damaged her car enough that she couldn't complete the race. As with every race team, Patrick's first Toyota Atlantic season also involved changes with her car, including switching engines, and changes in her crew.

By the last race of the season, Patrick had clearly sent the message that she was a strong competitor, ranking seventh among the 24 drivers in the series that year. Still, Patrick was hoping to earn a win to end her rookie season in Toyota Atlantic. "Being a rookie driver to the series on a rookie team has presented some problems, but I am pretty happy with how things have progressed," Patrick said. "I think we can have a strong weekend at Miami and finish the season the way we started, on the podium."

"NOT JUST A PRETTY FACE"

The last race of the season was the Argent Mortgage Toyota Atlantic 100k. It was held on the streets of Miami, Florida, on a temporary 1.15-mile loop that was closed to traffic, just like the track for the Toyota Celebrity/Pro Race that Patrick competed in and won in 2002.

In many racing series, the last race of the season is very important because sometimes there are so few points separating the drivers in first and second place that the last race decides who will be the season champion. In the 2003 Toyota Atlantic season, rookie A.J. Allmendinger had raced so well earlier in the year that it was clear he would be the season champion, even if he did not finish the race. But for the rest of the competitors, how they finished in the Miami race would very likely affect their final standing for the season. The closest two drivers in points were Patrick and series veteran Joey Hand. Hand was in sixth place, but Patrick was just five points behind him in seventh.

From the first round of qualifying at the Miami race, Patrick was going strong. She logged the fourth-quickest lap, but she still wasn't satisfied. "Fourth isn't bad, but I always want to do better," she said. After several rounds of qualifying, Patrick improved her lap times, but so did the other drivers. In final qualifying, she had the fifth-fastest time, meaning she would start fifth in the race.

When the Argent Mortgage Toyota Atlantic 100k began on September 28, 2003, the temperature was 84° Fahrenheit (29° Celsius), but it felt hotter than that because of high humidity. Many of the race teams looked at the cloudy sky over Miami and were concerned that rain might affect the race. The race began at 10:30 A.M., and immediately A.J. Allmendinger, who had won the pole position, began to have mechanical trouble and was forced to pull into the pits. By the second lap, Michael Valiante, who had started the race in third, and Patrick, who had started in fifth, passed Ryan Dalziel, who had started second. Valiante moved up to first place, and Patrick moved up to second place.

A few laps later, on the eighth lap, driver Marc Breuers lost control and spun into the barrier of tires that lined the track. His car's rear wing came loose in the crash, and driver Jonathan Macri hit it as it lay on the track. It took four laps for the safety crew to remove the debris from the track. During this time, called a caution period, all the drivers were required to slow down and keep their positions.

When the race restarted, on lap 12, Patrick accelerated rapidly, hoping to catch Valiante; but he began to pull farther and farther away. By lap 24, Valiante had a pretty big lead—about 2.6 seconds ahead of Patrick. By then, Patrick had another concern: the car right behind her, driven by Ryan Dalziel. He had been driving strong, and his car was just a little bit behind hers. He was looking for the opportunity to pass her and move into second place.

By lap 40, Patrick had not only been able to keep her car in second, but Dalziel had fallen behind. He was now

Second-place winner Danica Patrick looks on as Michael Valiante of Canada receives the trophy at the conclusion of the Toyota Atlantic Championship on September 28, 2003.

almost three seconds behind her. Just the same, Patrick was struggling to catch Valiante. By lap 51, he was more than five seconds ahead of Patrick. But it didn't remain

FROM TOYOTA TO INDYCARS

The Toyota Atlantic Championship series is the oldest development series in North America. A development series is one that prepares inexperienced drivers for the highest levels of professional racing. The Toyota Atlantic Series is designed especially to prepare drivers for the Champ Car World Series. In Danica Patrick's case, however, her team owner, Rahal Letterman Racing, made the decision that she should compete in IndyCar racing when she was ready to move to the next level.

fourth-place driver Bryan Sellers and Patrick (in fifth) passed them. As a result, Patrick crossed the finish line third. It was the third time she had been on the podium in six races. "This is what wins championships, never giving up," she said.

For the rest of the season, Patrick raced solidly, finishing in the top 5 in every race except one. Still, the two other drivers closest to her in points raced better, and Patrick ended the season in third place for the championship. Although she would have liked to win the championship as well as a race that year, Patrick won something else that season: the confidence of team owner Bobby Rahal.

Rahal was so impressed with Patrick's driving skills that, at a press conference for the 2004 Indianapolis 500, he announced that he was ready to put her in the race the following year, 2005. That surprised everyone, including Patrick. "This is the first time I've heard him say, 'She's ready to be here,'" she said. "I think I'm ready. If you can drive a race car, you can drive any race car. With a little bit of practice and knowledge of some of the characteristics of it, you can drive anything."

By the end of the 2004 season, Rahal's casual comment became a definite plan. In December, Rahal announced that Patrick would join her IndyCar teammates Buddy Rice and Vitor Meira on the Rahal Letterman Racing Indy Racing League team. Not only would Patrick compete in the 2005 Indianapolis 500, she would also race in all 17 IRL races. It was a big opportunity, and one that Rahal hoped Patrick could live up to. "Patrick is in a situation where she could be competitive," he said. "But ultimately, she's going to have to stand on the gas, and that's up to her."

5

THE BIG TIME

Patrick crashed in her first race of the 2005 IRL season; but despite that, she quickly proved that she was a strong competitor. She started second and finished fourth in the fourth race of the year, leading the race for 32 laps. That caught people's attention—people who then followed her into the next race, the Indy 500.

After the Indy 500, Patrick suddenly went from being a professional race car driver in the big leagues of open-wheel racing to an athlete with a celebrity-like status. People who weren't even racing fans knew Patrick's name in the same way that people who don't follow bicycling know Tour de France champion Lance Armstrong.

When Patrick arrived at the Texas Motor Speedway for the next race, she found herself surrounded by fans and media nearly everywhere she went. Sometimes they even followed her into the bathroom! At her autograph session, fans waited as long as 10 hours in line to get her autograph. Patrick was truly larger than life: A mural showing her on the cover of *Sports Illustrated* magazine was painted on a billboard outside the speedway. She was the first driver in the Indy 500 since 1981 to appear as the main photo subject on a cover of *Sports Illustrated*. She was now part of the big time.

Patrick's fellow drivers teased her about her newfound fame. At the driver's meeting before the Bombardier Learjet 500 race, Patrick's teammates Buddy Rice and Vitor Meira arrived wearing T-shirts that said, "Danica's Teammate"

A billboard featuring Danica Patrick on the cover of *Sports Illustrated* greeted race fans at the Texas Motor Speedway in Fort Worth, Texas, in 2005. The hand-painted mural bearing Patrick's likeness measured 20 by 40 feet.

and "Danica's Other Teammate." Rice gave driver Dan Wheldon a T-shirt that said, "I actually 'won' the Indy 500," making fun of the fact that Wheldon won the race, but Patrick got most of the publicity. Although the teasing was playful, Patrick's fellow drivers were all business on the track. Despite starting in third place, Patrick finished thirteenth. "These guys are incredible race car drivers out there, and I have a lot to learn," she said.

Learning was really what Patrick's rookie IRL season was all about. In the 17 races in the 2005 season, she had four accidents and one mechanical problem that took her out of a race early. She started in the first five positions nine times, including three pole positions, yet she finished in the top 5 just twice. Still, her performance on the track was strong enough to make her the Rookie of the Year.

The first time Patrick captured the pole position was at the Kansas Speedway, for the Argent Mortgage Indy 300. Her fastest lap of 214.668 mph qualified her to be first to

Danica Patrick (*left*) spins following a collision during the Toyota Indy 400, the Indy Racing League's season finale, on October 16, 2005, at California Speedway in Fontana, California.

start the race. Her time was just slightly faster than her teammate Rice's time of 214.650 mph, and Rice had won that race in 2004. Her other teammate, Vitor Meira, qualified third with a speed of 214.546 mph. The fact that the three teammates qualified in first, second, and third was unusual. The last time three drivers from the same team had qualified in the first three positions at an IRL race was in 2002.

Winning the pole position is very important to drivers, in part because they get extra money and points. Sometimes, but not always, it also gives them an advantage in the race. "On a big track like this it probably matters just a little bit less," Patrick explained. "There's the tow and people can draft behind you and go around you, so sometimes being the first person is not the best. But at least you're able to choose when you want to hit the gas when the green flies, and you can kind of control the start of the race. You don't have other cars in front of you changing the wind in front of the car."

Although she had the fastest time in qualifying, Patrick did not win the race as she had hoped. By the second lap, Patrick's teammate Rice had passed her, and then she began falling farther behind due to steering and mechanical problems with her car. When Patrick went in for a pit stop to try to correct some of the car's problems, her crew was very slow, and they lost precious seconds while the race leaders got farther ahead. Then, as Patrick was leaving pit lane, she nearly spun her car because her tires weren't gripping the ground tightly as they should.

She ended up placing ninth and was disappointed with her finish. She might have done better if it hadn't been for the problems with her car. As she described her car's problems to reporters after the race, she said, "Those

Danica Patrick leads teammate Buddy Rice through the first turn of the 2005 Argent Mortgage Indy 300 at the Kansas Speedway in Kansas City, Kansas.

aren't excuses, but it is that everything has to go right for you to win a race and today we didn't have everything fall into place."

HOMETOWN CROWD

Patrick captured the pole for the third time at the PEAK Antifreeze Indy 300 Presented by Mr. Clean at the Chicagoland Speedway on September 10, 2005. Her fastest lap speed was 215.970 mph, while her teammate Rice qualified second with a speed of 215.799 mph. For a moment, it looked as if Patrick would lose her pole position to driver Ryan Briscoe, who had a slightly faster qualifying lap. But then Briscoe's car did not pass the technical inspection after qualifying, and as a result his lap time was thrown out.

Patrick was thrilled with winning the pole position at a track so close to her hometown. "It is a great feeling to win the pole here at Chicago in front of so many friends and family," she said. "Three poles in a season is a great accomplishment for any driver and I am especially proud to have done it as a rookie."

With her third pole, Patrick tied the IRL record for the most pole positions won by a rookie. Tomas Scheckter, who would also be driving in this 2005 race, set that record in 2002. Although starting the race first is definitely an accomplishment, Patrick knew it was really about who finishes first. "All poles are great, but the reason we come to the track is to win the race," she said.

This time, when the race started, Patrick stayed in the lead for the entire first lap. Her lead didn't last for long, though, because Scheckter passed her on the second lap. On lap 28, an unusual thing happened: The race was stopped. A serious accident involving multiple cars had occurred on lap 20. After the accident was cleared, race officials realized that they needed to repair a portion of fence that was damaged in the crash, so they stopped the race for 17 minutes.

On lap 187, Patrick was in fourth place as the racers were driving under a caution flag. On lap 188 of the 200-lap race, Patrick thought she heard on her in-car radio that the race had restarted, so she stepped on the gas. Unfortunately, the race hadn't restarted, and Patrick was ordered to let two cars pass her as a penalty for starting too soon. The penalty left her in sixth position, which is where she finished the race.

Later, she explained her error. "On the last restart, I jumped the start because I thought I heard green, but now I don't think it was green," she said. "I have to blame myself for the error, though I thought I heard green on the radio. When I am in position to go for the win, I am going

Danica Patrick puts on her game face as she prepares to enter her car prior to the start of the 2005 PEAK Antifreeze Indy 300 at the Chicagoland Speedway in Joliet, Illinois. Patrick started from the pole position and finished sixth.

to be proactive and I was just trying to get a good jump and gain a spot or two."

As the 2005 season of IndyCar racing came to a close, Patrick remained the IRL's most popular driver. But she had also earned something more—the respect of her

GETTING PERSONAL

On November 19, 2005, Danica Patrick married Paul Hospenthal, a physical therapist. She met him in 2001 when Bobby Rahal sent her to Hospenthal's office after she injured her hip doing yoga. They couple lives in Scottsdale, Arizona, with their miniature schnauzer, Billy.

Paul Hospenthal shares the ride as his wife, Danica Patrick, waves to fans during a parade held before the 2006 Indianapolis 500.

fellow drivers. "I've always been respected, within reason, because of everything I've done," she said. "The real defining moment for me was after a practice during the first week at Indy when I was faster than everybody. [Tony] Kanaan and [Dario] Franchitti drove by in a golf cart and told me, 'Good job.' You can just tell that they were sincere. They respected me completely as a driver, and they know that I'm somebody they need to beat."

6

STAYING
WITH INDY

The year 2006 was Patrick's second season in the IRL, and it was a rough year from the start. During warm-ups for the very first race of the season, her teammate Paul Dana was killed in a crash. Devastated, team owner Rahal made the decision that Patrick and her teammate Buddy Rice would not compete in the race. Missing one of the 15 races that season meant that most likely Patrick and Rice wouldn't be contenders for the season championship because they would not be able to earn enough points to catch up to the leading drivers. It was a hard decision for Rahal to make, but one that Patrick agreed with. When a driver dies on the track, it is always hard for the other drivers, especially his teammates, to concentrate on the race. Rahal couldn't take the chance that Patrick or Rice might be hurt, too.

When she did finally compete, things were a bit challenging. At the Twin Ring Motegi race in Japan, Patrick started fourteenth and finished eighth. Although it was a respectable finish, it was nothing compared to 2005, when Patrick started second and finished fourth.

Danica Patrick (*in lead*) and teammate Buddy Rice compete at the Twin Ring Motegi 1.5-mile oval track in Motegi, Japan. Patrick came in eighth and Rice took fifth in the Bridgestone Indy Japan 300 race held on April 22, 2006.

In the next race, the Indy 500, Patrick also finished eighth, after starting tenth. It was a disappointment because in the 2005 race she led 19 laps and was a contender to win until she had fuel problems. Patrick said, "I guess I'm mad that we're eighth because we were running further up than that, and I think that if fuel strategy had bit some other people like it bit me last year, we could have ended up fourth or fifth." At the same time, Patrick was also pleased with her performance. "I didn't make any mistakes and the

Danica Patrick appears relaxed while meeting with photographers prior to the Camping World Grand Prix held at Watkins Glen International on July 8, 2007, near Watkins Glen, New York.

team didn't make any mistakes," she said, comparing the race to the one in 2005 when she stalled her car during a pit stop and was part of a small crash.

One of the reasons that Patrick didn't finish higher in the races was that the team was using an older **chassis** that wasn't as fast as the new Dallara chassis many of the others teams were using on their cars. In June, the team switched to the Dallara chassis, but things got worse for Patrick before they got better. For three races in a row, she didn't even finish in the top 10. It seemed the crew was having trouble making the needed adjustments to the new chassis that would help the car go fast.

Patrick grew frustrated. There was a lot of pressure on her to win her first race, and she had a car that wasn't very competitive. Patrick's contract with Rahal Letterman Racing was scheduled to end at the end of the year. She was considering switching to another team, or perhaps even leaving the Indy Racing League and competing in NASCAR's Nextel Cup or Formula One instead. Rumors swirled around Patrick for weeks as everyone wondered what she would do.

FACING THE FUTURE

On July 15, at the Firestone Indy 200 in Nashville, Tennessee, the crew's adjustments finally fell into place, and Patrick placed fourth. It was her best race of the season so far. "I'm proud of the team," she said. "We've had quite a long season so far. Indy was 10 times more difficult than last year. Obviously, changing over to the Dallara, we—mostly the pit crew—[have] been working [our] tails off in preparing these cars."

Rumors still flew about her plans for the next year. Then her new agreement was announced, after a race in Milwaukee, Wisconsin, at the end of July. Patrick would join Andretti Green Racing in 2007. Owned by former race car driver Michael Andretti, the team included two of the

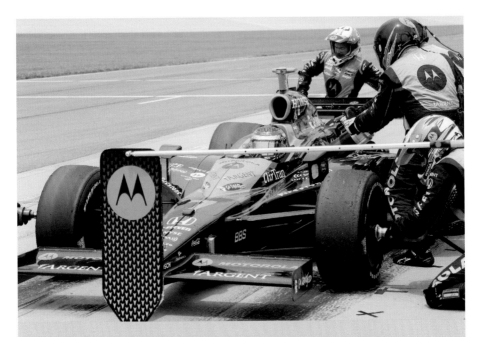

The Andretti Green pit crew services Danica Patrick's car during the Firestone Indy 200 at the Nashville Superspeedway in Lebanon, Tennessee, on July 15, 2007. Patrick started the race in seventh place and finished third.

strongest drivers in the Indy Racing League, Tony Kanaan and Dario Franchitti, as well as Michael's son Marco, who became the IRL's Rookie of the Year in 2006. "I'm excited to go to a team that has a lot of drivers I can learn from and knows how to win. They've been doing a lot of that," Patrick said.

For the rest of the race season, Patrick continued to struggle. She never finished higher than eighth place and, during one race, didn't finish at all because she ran out of fuel. At the end of the race season, Patrick began to work with her new team. She fit in right away, going out to dinner and text messaging her teammates. "Of course, not

KEEPING IN SHAPE

Because Patrick is one of the smallest race car drivers ever to compete in the sport, it is especially important that she is in top physical condition. To stay in shape, she runs, exercises with weights, and does bikram yoga (a kind of yoga that is done in a very hot room so performers get very sweaty). Although she exercises her entire body, Patrick focuses on her upper body strength the most because her upper half is what needs to be the strongest to pilot her race car.

only are they fantastic drivers, but they're also friends, so that's something new for me," she said.

Although Patrick said she would stay with IndyCars for the near future, she was still keeping the possibility open of racing in another series. "I don't know what's going to come next," she said. "I don't think I could have ever imagined where I was going to be if you were asking me five years ago. . . . I don't know what the future holds. It seems like it's moving at a fast pace for me. I just would hope it would bring me to a successful team or keep me at a successful team, whenever that was."

STATISTICS

2005 IRL SEASON

Location	Start	Finish	Laps Led	Winnings
Homestead-Miami Speedway	9	15	0	$36,000
Phoenix International Raceway	18	15	0	$36,000
Streets of St. Petersburg	15	12	0	$40,700
Twin Ring Motegi	2	4	32	$83,700
Indianapolis Motor Speedway	4	4	19	$378,855
Texas Motor Speedway	3	13	0	$38,500
Richmond International Raceway	21	10	0	$42,000
Kansas Speedway	1	9	0	$43,300
Nashville Superspeedway	2	7	9	$43,000
The Milwaukee Mile	6	19	0	$31,300
Michigan International Speedway	8	20	0	$30,600
Kentucky Speedway	1	16	0	$34,100
Pikes Peak International Raceway	5	8	0	$43,300
Infineon Raceway	16	20	0	$31,900
Chicago Speedway	1	6	1	$54,200
Watkins Glen International	16	16	0	$36,600
California Speedway	4	18	2	$33,600
TOTAL				$1,037,655

2006 IRL SEASON

Location	Start	Finish	Laps Led	Winnings
Homestead-Miami Speedway	17	17	0	$35,200
Streets of St. Petersburg	14	6	0	$50,200
Twin Ring Motegi	14	8	0	$68,900
Indianapolis Motor Speedway	10	8	0	$285,805
Watkins Glen International	16	8	0	$47,400
Texas Motor Speedway	14	12	0	$43,100
Richmond International Raceway	14	15	0	$38,900
Kansas Speedway	12	11	0	$44,400
Nashville Superspeedway	10	4	0	$65,500
The Milwaukee Mile	14	4	0	$65,500
Michigan International Speedway	11	17	0	$36,100
Kentucky Speedway	11	8	0	$47,400
Infineon Raceway	11	8	0	$49,000
Chicagoland Speedway	15	12	0	$43,100
TOTAL				$920,505

CHRONOLOGY

1982   Danica Sue Patrick is born on March 25.

1992   Competes in her first go-kart race.

1994   Wins first championship, the World Karting Association Grand National Championship in the Yamaha Sportsman class.

1996   Wins World Karting Association Manufacturers Cup National Points title in the Yamaha Junior and Restricted Junior classes.

1998   Moves to England to compete in Formula Vauxhall series, her first time racing open-wheel cars.

2000   Finishes second at the Formula Ford Festival in England, tying for the best finish ever by an American (besides Danny Sullivan, second in 1974.)

2002   Wins the Pro category of the Long Beach Grand Prix Toyota Pro/Celebrity race.

2003   Races first full season in professional racing in the United States in the Toyota Atlantic Championship; finishes sixth in the championship.

2004   Becomes first female driver to win a pole position in Toyota Atlantic racing; finishes third in Toyota Atlantic Championship; is the only driver that season to complete every lap.

2005   Races first full season in Indy Racing League; finishes twelfth in the championship; is named 2005 Bombardier Rookie of the Year and Indy 500 Rookie of the Year; marries Paul Hospenthal.

2006   Competes in her longest race ever, the Rolex 24 at Daytona, with codriver Rusty Wallace; finishes ninth in the championship; announces move to Andretti-Green Racing.

GLOSSARY

Accelerator—The foot pedal that controls the amount of power let into the engine; often called the "gas pedal."

CART (Championship Auto Racing Teams)—A professional racing series with open-wheel cars.

Caution flag—A yellow flag that is shown to the drivers to signal that there is an obstacle on the course, such as a crashed car, and to tell drivers to slow down.

Chassis—The frame, wheels, and machinery of a car, upon which the body sits.

Drafting—To follow another car around an oval track, closely enough to take advantage of the suction of air behind it; this allows both cars to go faster than each could on its own, while at the same time using less fuel and horsepower.

Formula One—A professional racing series with open-wheel cars.

Indy Racing League (IRL)—A professional racing series with open-wheel cars.

Midget—A small race car with an open cockpit, designed to race on an oval-shaped dirt or paved track that is usually one-fifth to one-half of a mile long.

Nose cone—The cone-shaped front end of an IndyCar.

Open-wheel—A type of car in which the wheels are not enclosed in metal protective structures called fenders, but instead are out in the open; "open-wheel racing" is racing that uses these kinds of cars.

Pit stop—A stop during a race to add fuel, change tires, or perform repairs.

Pole position—The starting position on the inside front row for a race. A driver who is "on the pole" is said to have an advantage because he or she has no other cars to pass to be in the lead.

Qualifying rounds—A system of timed practice runs held before races, used to establish which drivers are eligible for the race and to determine the drivers' positions on the starting grid.

Rookie—A race car driver competing in his or her first season in a particular racing series.

BIBLIOGRAPHY

Associated Press. "Patrick to Stay in IRL, but switch to Andretti Green." July 26, 2006.

Bernstein, Viv. "Humbled, Patrick Steers Focus to Veterans." *New York Times*, June 13, 2005.

CART Toyota Atlantic Championship. "Monterrey Saturday PM Press Notes." ChampCarAtlantic.com, March 22, 2003.

CART Toyota Atlantic Championship. "Monterrey Sunday PM Press Notes." ChampCarAtlantic.com, March 23, 2003.

CART Toyota Atlantic Championship. "Miami Friday Afternoon Press Notes." ChampCarAtlantic.com, September 26, 2003.

CART Toyota Atlantic Championship. "Miami Sunday Press Notes." ChampCarAtlantic.com, September 28, 2003.

Clark, Cammy. "Danica Patrick not shy about marketing herself as female driver." Knight-Ridder, September 27, 2003.

"Danica Patrick's Expectations for the 2007 Season." *Auto Racing Daily*, March 8, 2007.

"Danica Patrick fastest on carb day." DanicaRacing.com, May 27, 2005.

"Danica Patrick Gets Chance To Drive In IRL." *Vancouver Sun*, December 9, 2004.

"Danica Patrick seeks path to the top in 2002." AutoRacing1.com, April 1, 2002.

Gregory, Sean. "10 Questions for Danica Patrick." *Time*, Canadian edition, June 3, 2005.

Guthrie, Janet. Janet Guthrie: *A Life at Full Throttle.* Toronto, Canada: Sport Media Publishing, 2005.

Herman, Steve. "Danica Patrick Gets Surprise from Car Owner Bobby Rahal." AP Worldstream, May 25, 2004.

Indy Racing League. "Daily Trackside Report—July 2." IndyCar.com, July 2, 2005.

Lewandowski, Dave. "At end of hectic week, Patrick punches in fourth." Indycar.com, July 15, 2006.

"Patrick Brings Home Top-Ten Results for Rahal Letterman Racing." DanicaRacing.com, July 6, 2005.

"Patrick and Rice Sweep from Row at Chicagoland." DanicaRacing.com, September 10, 2005.

"Patrick Sixth at Chicagoland." DanicaRacing.com, September 11, 2005.

"Rahal Letterman Racing just misses Indy 500 win as Miera places 2nd, Patrick 4th in her rookie race." DanicaRacing.com, May 29, 2005.

St. James, Lyn. *Ride of Your Life: A Race Car Driver's Journey.* New York: Hyperion, 2002.

Stubbs, Dave. "Look out guys, here she comes." *Montreal Gazette*, August 23, 2003.

Team Rahal Letterman Racing Press Release. "Double Header Weekend Ahead for Rahal Letterman's Atlantic Team." ChampCarAtlantic.com, June 15, 2004.

Team Rahal Letterman Racing Press Release. "Patrick Looks to Duplicate Monterrey Success." ChampCarAtlantic.com, May 18, 2004.

Team Rahal Letterman Racing Press Release. "Qualifying Trouble Continues to Haunt Rahal Atlantic Duo." ChampCarAtlantic.com, July 2, 2004.

Team Rahal Letterman Racing Press Release. "Team Rahal—Miami Preview." ChampCarAtlantic.com, September 24, 2003.

Toyota Atlantic Championship Race Report. "Dalziel Continues Perfect Toyota Atlantic Weekend With Record-Setting Pole at Monterrey." ChampCarAtlantic.com, May 22, 2004.

Toyota Atlantic Championship Race Report. "Former Series Champion Fogarty Earns Second Consecutive Victory by Winning First of Two Toyota Atlantic Championship Races In Portland." ChampCarAtlantic.com, June 19, 2004.

Toyota Atlantic Championship Race Report. "Sunday Afternoon Pit Notes." ChampCarAtlantic.com, June 20, 2004.

Toyota Atlantic Championship Race Report. "Saturday Race Press Notes." ChampCarAtlantic.com, July 3, 2004.

"Toyota Pro/Celebrity Race 2002 Qualifying Notes & Quotes." Toyota Grand Prix of Long Beach Press Notes, undated.

Weir, Tom. "Danica plans to deliver at Indy." *USA Today*, May 23, 2005.

FURTHER READING

Braulick, Carrie A., *IndyCars*. Mankato, Minn.: Capstone Press, 2005.

Bledsoe, Glen, and Karen Bledsoe. *The World's Fastest IndyCars*. Mankato, Minn.: Capstone Press, 2003.

Guthrie, Janet. *Janet Guthrie: A Life at Full Throttle*. Toronto, Canada: Sport Media Publishing, 2005.

Indy-Tech Publishing. *Danica Patrick*. Indianapolis, Ind.: Indy-Tech Publishing, 2005.

Ingram, Jonathan. *Danica Patrick: America's Hottest Racer*. Osceola, Wisc.: Motorbooks, 2005.

Patrick, Danica, and Laura Morton. *Danica: Crossing the Line*. Parsippany, N.J.: Fireside, 2006.

Pimm, Nancy Roe. *Indy 500: The Inside Track*. Plain City, Ohio: Darby Creek Publishing, 2004.

Reed, Terry. *Indy: The Race and Ritual of the Indianapolis 500*. Dulles, Va.: Potomac Books, 2005.

Savage, Jeff. *Danica Patrick*. Minneapolis, Minn.: Lerner Publications, 2006.

Shaw, Jeremy. *Autocourse Champ Car Official Yearbook 2003–2004*. Osceola, Wisc.: Motorbooks, 2004.

St. James, Lyn. *Ride of Your Life: A Race Car Driver's Journey*. New York: Hyperion, 2002.

VIDEO

"The Season: Danica Patrick's Race for Indy." ESPN, June 11, 2005.

"Girl Racers." The Discovery Channel, September 2005.

WEB SITES

www.danicaracing.com
Official Web site of Danica Patrick.

www.danicafans.com
Web site created by a fan, with full information about Danica and links to articles and media appearances.

www.indycar.com
Official Web site of the Indy Racing League; statistics and news about all drivers in the league.

www.ikfkarting.com
Official Web site of the International Kart Federation and *Karter News* magazine.

www.gplb.com
Official Web site of the Toyota Grand Prix of Long Beach and the Long Beach Grand Prix Toyota Pro/Celebrity race.

www.andrettigreenracing.com
Official Web site of the Andretti Green Racing team; information about Danica Patrick and her teammates.

www.champcaratlantic.com
Official Web site of the Champ Car (formerly Toyota) Atlantic racing series; statistics, schedules, and driver information.

www.worldkarting.com
Official Web site of the World Karting Association and *Karting Scene* magazine.

PICTURE CREDITS

INDEX

ABOUT THE AUTHOR

TARA BAUKUS MELLO is a freelance automotive writer. During her 20 years as a writer, she has published more than 3,700 articles in newspapers and magazines. Baukus Mello is the author of *Tony Stewart, Rusty Wallace, Mark Martin, The Pit Crew, Stunt Driving,* and *Danica Patrick,* all part of Chelsea House's RACE CAR LEGENDS: COLLECTOR'S EDITION series. A graduate of Harvard University, she lives in Southern California, where she cruises the streets in her 1932 Ford pickup street rod that she built with her father.